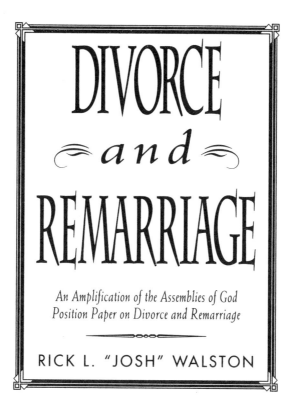

DIVORCE

and

REMARRIAGE

An Amplification of the Assemblies of God
Position Paper on Divorce and Remarriage

RICK L. "JOSH" WALSTON

D0925889

Gospel Publishing House
Springfield, Missouri
02–0502

To my parents (Lyle and Harriet), who demonstrated true
  marital commitment for forty-seven years
And to my wife Sue, a true blessing from the Lord

Table of Contents

Foreword

Many times I have wished I had a book like this to recommend to pastors and others who have called or written me with questions about divorce and remarriage.

Rick Walston as a young Assemblies of God minister saw a need. The questions raised by the increasing number of divorces and remarriages that plague our culture today gave him great concern, a concern many of us feel. It is a concern that is not going away, and we cannot ignore it.

This same concern had already led to the position paper, "Divorce and Remarriage," endorsed by the General Council of the Assemblies of God in August 1973. The subject is complex, however, and the position paper is brief. Many pastors have told me they still find it difficult to know how to apply the position paper in individual cases. In this book Walston attempts "to give an elucidation and expanded representation of the Assemblies of God perspective on the subject of divorce and remarriage."

It was my privilege to discuss the subject with the author while he was preparing a thesis for his master's degree. I found his insights helpful. Then because of the need we both saw, he went ahead and put his findings in book form.

The elucidation of this topic demands a careful study of what the Bible says as well as an explicit definition of terms. Walston does this. He makes it very evident that he has the highest regard for Scripture. He has also been careful to research and study what other Bible believers have said on the subject. He recognizes that there are good, Bible-believing people who have differences of opinion. But he shows that the Assemblies of God position is on solid ground. Those who disagree need to do as Walston has done: reexamine the biblical teachings in order to see the whole picture.

The book takes a positive stand and makes it clear that God is for marriage and against divorce. Marriage and the family are basic to God's provisions for human society. Both the Old and New Testaments show that. The Bible never takes a light view of these things. On the other hand, the Bible does not teach that divorce and remarriage are unpardonable sins. Therefore it is important to see what the Bible teaches about the nature of marriage, the nature of divorce, and the circumstances under which divorce and remarriage may or may not be allowed.

Readers should pay special attention to what this book has to say about each of the Bible passages that deal with divorce and remarriage. Note also what it shows to be the nature of fornication, the problem of polygamy, the matter of annulments, and the qualifications of elders (pastors) and deacons.

I commend Rev. Walston for his clear presentation and discussion of a difficult subject. May this book be a help to many.

STANLEY M. HORTON
DISTINGUISHED PROFESSOR OF BIBLE AND THEOLOGY
ASSEMBLIES OF GOD THEOLOGICAL SEMINARY

Acknowledgments

Acknowledgment is made to the following for permission to quote from the publications indicated:

Charisma, "Divorce Permitted but not Prescribed," by Richard Dobbins.

Fleming H. Revell Company, *The Right to Remarry,* by Dwight Hervey Small; *What the Bible Says About Marriage, Divorce and Remarriage,* by Edward G. Dobson.

Frank Cole, personal letter.

Glen Cole, *The Truth About Divorce and Remarriage.*

Moody Press, *Manners and Customs of Bible Lands,* by Fred H. Wight; *John MacArthur's Bible Studies on Divorce,* by John MacArthur.

Prentice Hall/A Division of Simon & Schuster, Inc., *Sex in the Bible,* by Michael R. Cosby.

SPCK, Holy Trinity Church, England, *The First Epistle to the Corinthians,* by C. K. Barrett.

Thomas Nelson Publishers, *An Expository Dictionary of Biblical Words,* by W. E. Vine, Merrill F. Unger, and William White, Jr.

Zondervan, *Marriage, Divorce, and Remarriage,* by Jay E. Adams.

Introduction

For finishing my master's degree in religion, the thesis application stipulated "experiences and/or involvements that have raised this theme for me and make it a present (both practical and academic) concern." As a minister with the Assemblies of God, I had dealt with persons who were divorced, trying to help them understand how it had affected their status within our denomination. The topic of divorce and remarriage from an Assemblies of God perspective was indeed a topic of experience and practical concern.

This topic is also of academic concern. Some time ago in a pastorate, I decided to teach my church about this subject. After doing some research, however, looking for a clear statement of the Assemblies of God position, I found only the August 1973 position paper this book is based on. (Glen Cole, Assemblies of God pastor of Capital Christian Center, has also published a sermon [©1982] on the subject.) I know of no other books or extensive studies expressing the Assemblies of God perspective. And it seems that too often very few Assemblies of God people, clergy included, have seen the position paper.

Though the position paper is a good piece of work, it is very brief. Therefore I have tried to "give meat" to it: Using its outline, I have simply expanded its main points. For those who would like to read the paper without commentary or interruption, its text is in Appendix B.

In wading through the many pages of material on this highly emotional subject, I have come across reliable scholars who disagree theologically with one another on this issue. These writers have seemingly good, solid arguments for their particular positions. But it has not been my purpose to respond to all those positions. Rather my goal has been to give an elucidation and expanded representation of the Assemblies of God perspective on the subject of divorce and remarriage, to reflect this position. If this study has done that accurately, it has achieved its purpose.

My purpose has also been to make this presentation understandable to laypeople as well as clergy. Therefore, I have purposely refrained from using much technical terminology; where such terms are used, explanations follow. Though I have tried to stay away from the argumentative rhetoric that I encountered so often in studying this subject, some of it has been retained in the refutation of ideas and the defense of others.

This study is admittedly eclectic. I have borrowed from various authors of differing theological presuppositions and various denominational backgrounds and traditions. Quotation of them in this study, however, does not indicate that the Assemblies of God accepts all their beliefs and teachings. At the same time, neither do those so quoted necessarily agree with all theology of the Assemblies of God—or even with the entirety of this study. Nevertheless, I do appreciate the various views, both those I included and those I did not. They have helped me formulate my own position on this volatile subject of divorce and remarriage.

I believe that both clergy and members of the Assemblies of God will benefit from this work by having a fuller understanding of the position held by their denomination.

Also, I hope that those who do not agree with the Assemblies of God position will read and reread this material so an intelligent interaction between differing viewpoints can occur. Prejudices are fostered by ignorance. I hope that this study will overcome some prejudices.

1

Marriage

Marriage is not a human idea or institution. Marriage originated in the mind of God. "God created man in His own image, in the image of God He created him; male and female He created them" (Genesis 1:27). As stated in the Assemblies of God position paper on divorce and remarriage: "A basic human relationship, marriage is God-ordained."[1]

The marriage relationship is social. The position paper, speaking of Adam and Eve, the first marriage, states: "Their relationship was to be social as well as physical. 'The Lord God said, it is not good that the man should be alone; I will make him a help meet for him' (Genesis 2:18)" (p. 5). The union of the two persons creates the smallest unit of society.[2] This social unit, referred to in Scripture as a house or household (Genesis 7:1; Deuteronomy 11:6; Joshua 2:19; John 4:53; Acts 10:2; 16:31; 18:8), is foundational to all society.

Since this is the case, the Assemblies of God holds that the home (or marriage) is a most sacred institution and is to be highly honored. One of the wedding ceremonies in the Assemblies of God *Minister's Manual,* observes, "Of the world's three great institutions—the home, the church, and the state—the home is the oldest and most sacred."[3] When the institution of marriage is weakened by divorce, society as a whole is weakened and in trouble. For, as Jay Adams says, "The attack on marriage, experienced today, is actually an attack on society itself (and on God, who built society on marriage)" (p. 4).

God-ordained Marriage

Since marriage was created, ordained, and instituted by God, His design should not be contradicted by an imposition of rules or regulations. If they are of human origin, they must be in harmony with God's purpose for marriage.

Only a few rules and regulations surround marriage. Foremost among them is that marriage is to be the legal union of only two persons, a man and a woman, for life. Someone has pointed out that when God created mankind, He began with only two humans, not three or four. There were no spares in case the relationship between Adam and Eve just didn't work out. Dwight Hervey Small states,

> Immediately following the creation of Eve and her union with Adam, we read in Genesis 2:24: "Therefore a man leaves his father and his mother and cleaves to his wife, and they become one flesh." The Creation orders are suited to mankind before the Fall. Marriage was designed to be indissoluble, an enduring relationship through life. A growing unity was to characterize marriage so as to make it a total union of persons in a common life. The concept of *one flesh* brought together all the components of personal life. Marriage was a complementary union in which both husband and wife were completed by the other.... Without the forces of evil to disrupt this union, Adam and Eve represented the ideal of marriage without the possibility of divorce. No provision for divorce and remarriage was made a valid part of the orders of Creation. It was to this that Jesus referred in Matthew 19:8: "... but from the beginning it was not so." He pointed to God's original intention, an intention which had not changed.[4]

Ideally marriage is dissolved only by death (Romans 7:2–3). A key thought in the mind of God about the permanency of marriage is revealed in Genesis 2:24. The Hebrew word for "cleave" (or "united," NIV) in this verse is *dabaq* which, according to W. E. Vine, means "to cling, cleave, keep close. Used in modern Hebrew in the sense of 'to stick to, adhere to,' *dabaq* yields the noun form for 'glue' and also the more abstract ideas of 'loyalty, devotion.' "[5] In Matthew 19:5, Jesus uses the Greek word *kollao* ("cleave," "united") to denote the idea of indissolubility. According to Vine, *kallao* means "to join fast together, to glue, to cement" (p. 188). God's intended permanency and indissolubility of the marriage relationship are clearly seen in these words.

Polygamy

Polygamy is a recognized fact of the Old Testament. Although the Law forbade polygamy for the kings of Israel (Deuteronomy 17:17), both Solomon and David had many wives—and much trouble as a result.[6] Polygamy, however, was not forbidden for the average Israelite. "Deuteronomy considers polygamy an acceptable practice, offering neither encouragement nor condemnation for it."[7]

Nevertheless, God's ideal marriage is an exclusive relationship between one man and one woman. When pressed by the Pharisees for an answer to the divorce "command" of Moses, Jesus clearly stated that God's ideal is monogamy (Matthew 19:4–8; position paper, p. 6). For two people to attain a oneness of physical, emotional, intellectual, and spiritual being, they must commit themselves exclusively to one another. This ideal state of oneness cannot be attained within a polygamous relationship.[8] Michael Cosby seems to confirm this truth when he states,

> Although polygamy is perfectly acceptable in the society proposed by Deuteronomy, difficulties arising from polygamous marriages are recognized. For example, if the husband loves one of his wives a lot more than the other(s), intense problems might arise due to the favoritism he might show to her and her children. A good

> illustration of this may be seen in Genesis 29:15 to 30:24. This is a story filled with pathos, describing the great pain experienced by Leah because Jacob loved his other wife, Rachel, much more. Leah repeatedly sought to gain Jacob's favor by bearing children for him, but she was never able to win his love. Jacob's favoritism also caused interfamily conflict among his children, for Leah's sons resented the favored status of Rachel's sons. (P. 17)

According to Fred H. Wight, the Old Testament implicitly favors monogamy. First, this may be seen in the narratives of unhappy homes due to polygamy. Often rivalry between wives of the same husband occurs, for example, Leah and Rachel (Genesis 30), Hannah and Peninnah (1 Samuel 1:1–6). "Second, monogamy among religious leaders and certain outstanding characters sets the right example for the masses. Men like Adam, Noah, Isaac, Joseph, Moses, and Job had but one wife. Also the high priest (Lev. 21:14) and the prophets were, as far as we know, monogamous" (pp. 124–125).

The ideal marriage relationship in God's sight is "a lifelong monogamous union" (position paper, p. 6).

Heterosexual Marriages Only

A God-ordained marriage is made up of only members of the opposite sex. When I pastored in Longview, Washington, evangelist Dennis Nissley spoke at the church. One of his lines was, "God created Adam and Eve, not Adam and Steve!" The implication is obvious: God did not intend, nor does he condone, homosexual marriages.[9] Reverend Nissley's remark, and thus implication, is an accurate reflection of the Assemblies of God view of homosexual marriages: They are not legal, binding, or in or of the will of God.[10]

This position is also maintained by Edward Dobson in his book *What the Bible Really Says About Marriage, Divorce and Remarriage.* He states,

Society's movement toward a unisex concept of men and women is contradictory to God's creative intent. Society's increasing acceptance of homosexual and lesbian marriages as legitimate is in clear violation of Scripture. Men and women are different physically and emotionally. These differences must be recognized and accepted as ingredients for a successful marriage.[11]

A man and a woman committed to each other physically, emotionally, intellectually, and spiritually for life was God's intent at creation and is still his intent today.

The Covenant of Marriage

Marriage is much more than simply two persons deciding to live together under the blessing of the law. Marriage is a covenant: "The Lord has been a witness between you and the wife of your youth . . . she is your companion and your wife by covenant" (Malachi 2:14; see also Proverbs 2:17 and Ezekiel 16:8). The Hebrew word for covenant is *berith*, meaning "covenant; league; confederacy" (Vine, p. 82). This word is used in the Old Testament of agreements between men. David and Jonathan had such an agreement, having to do with mutual protection not only between them but their descendants as well:

And Jonathan made a covenant with David because he loved him as himself. . . . Jonathan said to David, "Go in peace, for we have sworn friendship with each other in the name of the Lord, saying, 'The Lord is witness between you and me, and between your descendants and my descendants forever'" (1 Samuel 18:3; 20:42, NIV).

Marriage is an awesome responsibility. God is the witness of the covenant, and in the case of divorce he will call the responsible party into account. Therefore, "marriage is a covenant, a solemn binding agreement made before God and man" (position paper, p. 6).

2

Divorce

God hates divorce. During a time in Israel's history when the men were divorcing their wives simply to marry foreign women, the prophet Malachi said,

> And this is another thing you do: you cover the altar of the Lord with tears, with weeping and with groaning, because he no longer regards the offering or accepts it with favor from your hand. Yet you say, "For what reason?" Because the Lord has been a witness between you and the wife of your youth, against whom you have dealt treacherously, though she is your companion and your wife by covenant. But not one has done so who has a remnant of the Spirit. And what did that one do while he was seeking a godly offspring? Take heed then, to your spirit, and let no one deal treacherously against the wife of your youth. For I hate divorce, says the Lord, the God of Israel, and him who covers his garment with wrong, says the Lord of hosts. So take heed to your spirit, that you do not deal treacherously (Malachi 2:13–16).

This type of divorce that is called treacherous in this passage is one that has absolutely no grounds for justification (Small, p. 40). The wives whom these men were divorcing had not committed adultery. The passage does not even record that they had burnt their husband's toast. These men simply decided to send away their wives because they had found other women more appealing. This then is a treacherous divorce and God states unequivocally that he hates it.

Among other reasons for God's loathing divorce is the pain

that divorce inevitably brings to everyone involved. Dr. Richard Dobbins points out that God hates divorce because of the great amount of hurt that all involved must endure. However, the divorcee remains the object of God's love. In other words, to put it in familiar words, God hates the sin, but He loves the sinner.[1] As Today's English Version states it, " 'I hate it when one of you does such a cruel thing to his wife' " (Malachi 2:16).

God also hates divorce because it is the breaking of a covenant, the breaking of one's vows.

Still another reason, as reflected in Malachi, is because divorce does not gender a holy offspring. "It hinders the growth of a 'godly seed' [Malachi 2:15b]. Broken homes do not tend to produce the healthiest offspring" (position paper, p. 8). They are more susceptible to evil than children of godly parents. For example, 30 years ago it was pointed out that "Of [the] 45 million children of school age in the nation 12 million come from homes broken by divorce or death. Of children charged with infractions of the law 85 percent come from these broken homes."[2] In just two consecutive years of the mid-80s there were almost 2.5 million divorces.[3] One's mind reels when considering the present divorce rate as a contributing factor to infractions of the law. The potential for crime by the lack of a "godly seed" is staggering. God says, with reason, "I hate divorce."

What God Has Joined Together

As has been established, God's intention was that marriage be indissoluble. Jesus, in confirmation of this ideal, states that when two people have come together in the marriage covenant relationship, they become one flesh, and "What therefore God has joined together, let no man separate" (Matthew 19:6). Jesus of course was speaking to the Pharisees, but his command, let no man separate what God has joined together, is just as binding today.

The question may arise, Are all marriages the joining together of God? This is a question whose attention is off-center. God joins a man and a woman who have left father and mother and have come together as spouses. That is, when two people make the commitment of marriage, *then* God joins them together as one flesh. And it is that "one flesh" Jesus commands that no one separate. This statement by Jesus also implies that marriage is not simply a legal contract involving two parties but a covenant involving three parties: the man, the woman, and God himself—the "surgeon" who joins the two.

This one flesh concept is illustrated in Adam and Eve. Originally they were one person; that is, Eve was taken from Adam's side. So even though they were physically separate, in a sense they had been/were still one flesh. This oneness is what God returns a man and woman to when they marry. In creation, woman was taken *from* man, and in marriage God places her back *with* man. Just as the Church is both body and bride of Christ, so the woman becomes both body and bride of the man. (See Ephesians 5:21–31.) That is not to imply that only the woman becomes one with the man; the man becomes one with the woman as well. This intricacy is wrought by God, and mankind is commanded, even warned, not to separate this holy union.

Old Testament Legislation of Divorce

The Old Testament clearly recognizes the fact of divorce. It was happening. Because it was happening and people were getting hurt, God gave laws to regulate it. "In giving Israel the law, God accepted people where they were, put restrictions on their wrong practices, and tried to direct them" (position paper, p. 8). The restriction, or regulation, of divorce in Deuteronomy seems to be a protection clause for the woman. The following verses have been separated for clarification (versification included):

> [1]When a man takes a wife and marries her, and it happens that she finds no favor in his eyes because he has found some indecency in her, and he writes her a certificate of divorce and puts it in her hand and sends her out from his house,
>
> [2]and she leaves his house and goes and becomes another man's wife,
>
> [3]and if the latter husband turns against her and writes her a certificate of divorce and puts it in her hand and sends her out of his house, or if the latter husband dies who took her to be his wife,
>
> [4]then her former husband who sent her away is not allowed to take her again to be his wife, since she has been defiled; for that is an abomination before the Lord, and you shall not bring sin on the land which the Lord your God gives you as an inheritance (Deuteronomy 24:1–4).

The restrictive portion of this passage is located in verse 4. Verses 1–3 simply document what it was that hard-hearted men were doing (Adams, p. 62). When a man takes and marries a wife, and when he finds something he does not like about her, and when he gives her a certificate of divorce, and when she gets remarried to another man, and when that other man divorces her or he dies, *then* . . . The *then* of verse 4 is the beginning of the restriction. Then the first husband cannot remarry the woman.

This restriction protected the woman from a hasty divorce by, perhaps, an angry or capricious husband. As Jay Adams says, without the prohibition of remarriage after the wife had married someone else, a husband might have divorced his wife with the thought, "If I'm wrong, I'll just remarry

Mary, if and when she becomes available again or if I can induce her to leave her second husband and return to me" (p. 62). God was protecting the woman from a man's putting her through such shame and humiliation. "Serial and trial marriages and divorces, with the possibility of return if one later happened to change his/her mind, were not permitted. One had to think twice before committing himself to the almost certain finality that divorce had in the culture under that regulation" (Adams, p. 31).

Moses and Divorce

The Pharisees thought that Moses had *commanded* divorce for certain situations, so when Jesus reiterated God's ideal, they asked him, "Why then did Moses *command* to give her a certificate and divorce her?" (Matthew 19:7; emphasis added). Jesus made it clear to them that Moses only *permitted* divorce—and that was only because of the hardness of men's hearts. As Richard Dobbins has observed, God may permit divorce, under certain circumstances, but he does not prescribe it (p. 15). Furthermore, even this permission was not for just "any cause at all" (Matthew 19:3), as was the thought and practice of most of the people of the day.

The question of what it was for which Moses allowed or permitted a man to divorce his wife is a difficult one to answer. For the answer to this question is an enigma and, one supposes, shall always remain so. The answer hinges upon the obscure Hebrew term *erwat debar* found in Deuteronomy 24:1. According to scholars, this term is not hard to translate, but it is hard, if not impossible, to interpret. An agreed upon translation is "a matter of nakedness." Jay Adams says that *erwat debar*

> seems to cover anything and everything (in this case)
> a husband might deem repugnant, and that he might

come to "dislike" [lit., "not find favor"] in his wife, so that he might determine to divorce her. (P. 62)

Edward G. Dobson says of *erwat debar:*

I believe it indicates some type of serious, shameful, and disgraceful conduct associated with sexual activity, but less than adultery. (P. 38)

Michael Cosby says that

in this particular situation it appears to indicate some sort of shameful action or condition and may be intentionally broad in scope, allowing for any number of possible situations. (P. 19)

The Assemblies of God position paper states:

The passage literally says that when a man divorces his wife "because he has found in her an unclean matter [a Hebrew word connected with uncovered stools (Deuteronomy 23:12–14), with Noah's nakedness (Genesis 9:21–23), and with Edom under the figure of a drunken woman (Lamentations 4:21)—that is, some moral or sexual uncleanness apart from adultery . . .]" (P. 9)

The ambiguity of this term was a point of disagreement between the two rabbinic schools of thought that had arisen by the time of Jesus, represented by Hillel and Shammai. Hillel and his followers were very liberal in their interpretation of *erwat debar.* They taught that it referred to anything that displeased the husband:

In the first part of the Talmud, the Jewish civil and religious law, some grounds for divorce according to the school of Hillel were: violation of the law of Moses or of Jewish customs, such as the woman causing her husband to eat food on which a tithe had not been paid;

> not setting apart the first dough; appearing in public
> with disheveled hair; spinning and exposing her arms
> in public; conversing indiscriminately with men; speak-
> ing disrespectfully of her husband's parents in his pres-
> ence; brawling in the house; or spoiling a dish for him.
> (Dobson, p. 35)

A stricter school of thought (which had less of a following) was led by Shammai. The school of Shammai was much more conservative in their interpretation of *erwat debar.* According to them it referred to unfaithfulness in marriage, serious sexual sin (Dobson, pp. 34–35).

In answer, the Hillelites pointed out that stoning was the prescribed measure for adultery at the time of Moses—not divorce. Therefore, *erwat debar* could not mean adulterous behavior because for that offense the law required death; it must have meant something less.

Today, fortunately, people facing divorce and desiring to know the biblical position are not at the mercy of the ambiguous phrase *erwat debar.* They need only to focus on Jesus' words. He ended the debate of interpretations and spoke clearly to the issue. The Assemblies of God interprets Jesus' words as meaning that divorce is "contrary to God's will and Word. He made this clear in Matthew 19:5–6 and Mark 10:6–9" (position paper, p. 10), verses we will look at more closely later.

3

Paul on Divorce

Questions have been raised about Paul making a distinction between what he says and what the Lord says.[1] Because of that distinction, some commentators have suggested that what Paul says is not inspired Scripture. But Paul has a reason for making such a distinction.

All through the Book of Romans Paul quotes from the Old Testament to prove his points. Galatians is another masterpiece of this strategy. Paul does this with all of his theology. Thus, he could be expected to quote chapter and verse and/or Jesus himself concerning the subject of divorce and remarriage, and this he does. In 1 Corinthians 7:10 Paul wrote: "Unto the married I command, *yet not I, but the Lord,* let not the wife depart from her husband" (emphasis added). Paul says that he received that word from the Lord (cf. Matthew 5:32; 19:4–9). As long as Jesus had given guidelines and laws concerning divorce and remarriage, Paul was obligated to quote him.

But when there was something about the subject of divorce and remarriage that Jesus had not expressly dealt with, Paul, as an inspired writer of Holy Writ, would have to pen guidelines for such instances (position paper, p. 10). This is exactly what he does in 1 Corinthians 7:12. In this verse Paul says, "But to the rest I say, not the Lord ... " Paul is not saying that what he is about to teach is not of God. What he is saying, in effect, is that no precedent exists, no previous Word from God, to cite on this subject. Thus he, by the unction and inspiration of the Holy Spirit, will now write. The Assemblies of God accepts Paul's "I say" as inspired Scripture on par with any and all other Scripture throughout the Bible. With that distinction Paul's teaching on the subject of divorce is made clearer.

No Divorce for Christian Couples

Speaking to Christian couples Paul says that the wife is not to leave her husband and a husband is not to send away his wife; there is to be no divorce (1 Corinthians 7:10–11). "The prohibition of separation and divorce (between Christians) seems to be absolute" (Barrett, p. 162). Paul gives this directive undoubtedly upon the authority of Jesus' own words (Cosby, 128–130). Paul, being a realist, recognized that even though there was a clear word from Jesus on the issue—no divorce—some Christians were still getting divorced. That fact did not give license, however. Paul says if a Christian couple do divorce, both are to remain single, allowing for the possibility of reconciliation. The divorced Christian has no option to remarry, unless of course it is to the ex-spouse (Barrett, p. 183).

Assemblies of God Pastor Glen Cole explains it with conviction:

> In Chapter 7[:10–11], Paul speaks to the married believers. A Christian does not divorce his or her companion! Exclamation mark. Period. The end! Verses 10 and 11: A Christian does not divorce . . . !

> If a Christian does divorce, they have two options, and only two options. Verse 11: "Let her remain divorced, or let her be reconciled to her husband."

> Also in verse 11, "Let not the husband put away his wife."

> Paul was not dealing with adultery. He was dealing with the "I want out" syndrome. That syndrome is now a part of the church.

So, with just as much authority as the apostle Paul,
I say, "Married believers do not divorce!"

It is not even a thought! God hates divorce. Malachi
2:18 says so. God hates divorce.[2]

Christians Forbidden to Initiate Divorce

After speaking to the Christian couples, Paul shifts his
attention to *the rest.* "But to the rest I say, not the Lord,
that if any brother has a wife who is an unbeliever, and she
consents to live with him, let him not send her away. And
a woman who has an unbelieving husband, and he consents
to live with her, let her not send her husband away"
(1 Corinthians 7:12–13).

As Christianity spread, more and more Gentiles were con-
verted, but the spouses of these new converts did not always
become Christians. Consequently, many Gentile Christians
were married to unbelieving spouses. In the New Testament
period this was something new: Jesus had not had to deal
with mixed-faith marriages (believer and non-believer) in
his teaching; His ministry had occurred largely within Ju-
daism (Barrett, p. 7). Thus, Paul is now called upon, as a
writer of inspired Scripture and "the apostle to the Gentiles"
(Romans 11:13, NIV) to deal with mixed unions. "The rest"
are the couples who are unequally yoked together, believers
married to unbelievers.

From what Paul says to this particular group, it appears
that the Corinthians had asked him specifically about sev-
eral issues, one of which is mixed-faith marriages. "The
question some of the Corinthian Christians were puzzling
over was, Does marriage to a nonbeliever defile the believer
and the children?" (Cosby, p. 130). According to Paul's heritage, a heritage which taught that for a Jew to be married
to a Gentile was to defile oneself and the offspring (Cosby,
p. 131), one might expect him to answer the Corinthians'

question by saying, Yes, it does defile! Yet, Paul does not say that at all. In fact, Paul says just the opposite: "The unbelieving husband is sanctified through his wife, and the unbelieving wife is sanctified through her believing husband; for otherwise your children are unclean, but now they are holy" (1 Corinthians 7:14).

Commenting on this passage, Glen Cole states: "It only takes one Christian to make a Christian home!" (p. 11). John Calvin wrote, "The godliness of the one does more to 'sanctify' the marriage than the ungodliness of the other to make it unclean."[3] Paul gives two reasons Christians should stay in a mixed-faith marriage: (1) The unbelieving spouse is sanctified by the believing spouse; (2) the children are sanctified by the presence of the Christian parent. Upon this basis Paul says that a Christian is not to initiate a divorce.

If a brother or sister is married to an unbeliever and the unbeliever is happy to remain in the marriage, then the Christian is obligated to remain married to him/her. Paul's commitment to the indissolubility of marriage is affirmed in his counsel for a believer to stay married to an unbeliever.

If the Unbeliever Departs

Paul gave different instructions for those Christians whose unbelieving spouses wanted a divorce. "If the unbelieving one leaves, let him leave; the brother or the sister is not under bondage in such cases, but God has called us to peace" (1 Corinthians 7:15). Commenting on this verse the Assemblies of God position paper states: "Thus, Paul indicates that the Christian cannot stop an unbelieving partner from leaving (getting a divorce) if he or she insists on it" (p. 11). If the unbeliever decides to leave and thus end the marriage, the believing partner is to let the spouse go.

There has been some question about how to interpret the partner's leaving. Some have suggested that something less than legal divorce is intended (Barrett, p. 168). Others (including the Assemblies of God) believe that what is meant in this passage by the leaving of the unsaved spouse is nothing less than legal divorce (Dobson, p. 79).

W. E. Vine says this word "leaves" ("depart," KJV) comes from the Greek word *chorizo* and means "to put apart, . . . to separate oneself, to depart from . . . marital affairs" (p. 266). The significance here is that the unbeliever "actually leaves" (*Williams New Testament*). The believer does not put the spouse away, but rather the unbeliever separates from the believer. Thus, if an unbelieving partner insists on divorce, it is a legal divorce, and the Christian is free in such cases.

4

Jesus on Divorce

Clearly Jesus referred to an acceptable reason for a Christian initiating divorce, often called the exception clause (see Matthew 5:32; 19:9). Jesus stated unequivocally that it is unlawful to divorce one's spouse *except* for fornication. The Assemblies of God position paper says that, "Jesus permitted a Christian to initiate a divorce when fornication was involved" (p. 11). The Christian is not bound to the marriage covenant when the partner has *already broken* that covenant through fornication; thus the Christian is permitted to divorce. For as the position paper points out:

> We must ... keep in mind that under the law the penalty for adultery was death. This penalty of death was given not to break the marriage relationship, but in recognition that it was already broken. (P. 15)

However, one must beware of seeing in the words of Jesus—like the Pharisees saw in the words of Moses (cf. Matthew 19:7; Deuteronomy 24:1–4)—a *command* to divorce. For Jesus has not commanded the Christian to divorce the unfaithful spouse. The whole message of the gospel is that a person can be forgiven when truly repentant. Likewise, the spouse of the unfaithful partner should forgive the offending party. The highest ideal and will of God is that repentance, forgiveness, and reconciliation occur between the couple, not divorce.

Nevertheless, repentance and forgiveness may not always result in restoration of the marriage. A spouse may feel unable to trust the offender again, that the two of them can never regain the commitment and intimacy they once knew.

Fornication Defined

Since divorce is biblically ethical only on the grounds of fornication, it is imperative to discover the definition of "fornication." The word under investigation in this passage is the Greek word *porneia*. The King James Version of the Bible translates it "fornication"; *The Bible in Basic English*, "loss of . . . virtue"; The New International Version, "marital unfaithfulness"; and the New American Standard Version, "unchastity."

In English, fornication has a rather narrow meaning. It is generally understood to be sexual relations between unmarried persons (by mutual consent). Because fornication does not involve married persons, it is commonly distinguished from adultery. However, the Greek word *porneia* in Matthew 5:32 and 19:9 has a much broader definition. Therefore, we must be careful to see the word in its biblical setting, not in our American setting.

> In American law, the word *fornication* has come to mean sexual sin by unmarried persons, over against *adultery*, which means sexual sin involving a married person. However, *that distinction must not be read back into the Bible* as many unwittingly do. It was not the biblical distinction. (Adams, p. 54)

Turning to W. E. Vine's *Expository Dictionary of Biblical Words* for a definition of *porneia*, one finds: "*Porneia* is used of illicit sexual intercourse . . . and it stands for, or includes, adultery" (p. 455).

Once the meaning of the Greek word *porneia* is understood, it becomes obvious that a much broader definition must be employed. Those who argue for the narrower "fornication" as opposed to the more general "unchastity" often give the cultural account that during Jesus' day a man would pay a dowry for a virgin bride. If either during the engagement or after the marriage he found her not to be a virgin due to sexual misconduct (fornication) before their marriage, he would have the right to divorce her (Dobson, p. 64). He had *paid* for a virgin but did not receive one. Therefore, the covenant of marriage was made null and void. This is an accurate assessment of Matthew 5:32 and 19:9—as far as it goes.

However, the Assemblies of God sees the application of this term extending far beyond this narrow interpretation, for it is employed in the New Testament to mean much more than fornication. As Glen Cole states,

> Fornication is not just the sinful act of single people. Fornication encompasses *all* sexual wrongs: homosexuality, lesbianism, adultery—*anything* that comes under sexual sin. (P. 10)

Adultery, Incest, and Homosexuality

First Corinthians 5 contains the account of a man who was having sexual relations with "his father's wife." The Greek word employed for this conduct is *porneia,* which the King James Version translates "fornication." This is the same Greek word as in Matthew 5:32; 19:9, which is also translated "fornication." But notice with whom this man was engaging in sexual relations—his father's wife. Taking it at face value, if this woman is the biological mother, then the fornication is incest. Many commentators, however, assume that this woman is the stepmother (see Today's English Version). If this is so, then the fornication taking place is adultery. Dobson sees this passage as covering both aspects: "In 1 Corinthians 5:1, Paul defines *fornication* as an incestuous and adulterous relationship" (p. 65). In either case, it cannot be "fornication" as defined by American usage.

John MacArthur states emphatically,

> The word "fornication" (Gk., *porneia*) is commonly used to encompass adultery. For example, 1 Corinthians 10:8 says, "Neither let us commit fornication (Gk., *porneia*), as some of them committed, and fell in one day three and twenty thousand." Now some people say, "It's talking about fornication there, not adultery. It's referring to sex outside of marriage." They're saying, then, that all twenty-three thousand people who were killed by God were unmarried. That's silly! Obviously, the word encompasses both sex outside of marriage and sex that would be constituted as adultery. Paul is not referring only to unmarried Israelites or unmarried Corinthians. The word encompasses all sexual evil.[1]

In Jude 7, the writer speaks of the "fornication" of Sodom and Gomorrah. The sin of the people of these cities is often seen as homosexuality. Barrett explains the variety of meanings in the term fornication *(porneia):* "In the New Testament ... it is regularly used for unchastity and sexual irregularity of almost any kind" (p. 121).

The Assemblies of God position paper states:

> The Greek work for "fornication" *(porneia)* may include especially repeated acts of adultery, but usually means habitual sexual immorality of any kind, both before and after marriage. (A *porne* was a prostitute.) A few scholars would limit the meaning of fornication here to incest, but this is not the normal usage of the word. (P. 11)

Thus the word *porneia,* translated "fornication" in the King James Version of the Bible, has in its scope illicit sexual relations between any persons, single or married. Therefore, according to Jesus, "marital unfaithfulness" (NIV) is grounds for divorce (Matthew 5:32; 19:9); the Christian has permission to initiate divorce if the spouse has been unfaithful to the marriage covenant through sexual misconduct.

Even so, it is best if the offended person can find the grace and the strength to forgive the offending spouse. For God's will remains repentance, forgiveness, and reconciliation.

5

Remarriage: Restrictions

The Scripture is clear about remarriage after one's spouse has died: "If her husband dies, she is free from the law, so that she is not an adulteress, though she is joined to another man" (Romans 7:3). In fact, remarriage in some instances is encouraged by Paul: "I want the younger widows to get married, bear children, keep house, and give the enemy no occasion for reproach" (1 Timothy 5:14). Remarriage in and of itself is not wrong. Jay Adams points out:

> The Book of Ruth is a good example of how favorably the Scriptures look upon remarriage. It is noteworthy that a whole book deals with this question, and that in the lineage (including Ruth) of Christ there are remarried persons. (P. 79)

There are qualifications on the divorced remarrying, however. The passage in Deuteronomy 24:1–4 speaks of remarriage in a matter-of-fact style. It entertains no questions of whether or not the divorced person would remarry, it is assumed. "The Law accepted the fact that divorce permitted remarriage" (position paper, p. 12).

Deuteronomy shows how clearly the Law permitted remarriage. "When a man takes a wife and he writes her a certificate of divorce and sends her out from his house, and she leaves and becomes another man's wife . . ." (Deuteronomy 24:1–2). Besides containing no debate about remarriage, this passage does not even try to discourage it. To this point, it seems to place no restrictions on the remarriage.

In fact, though the first marriage would have been arranged, the second marriage could be by personal choice.

> The divorced woman, like the widow, was her own person. She could return to her father's house, but need not. . . . She then [after divorce] had the right to give herself in marriage, whereas as a maiden, before her maturity, she was given in marriage by her father. (Small, pp. 32–33)

Scriptural Restrictions

Nevertheless, remarriage does have some scriptural restrictions. The passage in Deuteronomy goes on to say that if the divorced woman remarries another man and the second husband dies or divorces her, she cannot be remarried to her first husband (Deuteronomy 24:3–4).

Some people today teach that if those who are divorced and remarried want to become right with God, they must go back to their first marriage. This is clearly a violation of the Deuteronomy passage. Glen Cole gets rather impassioned when it comes to this subject:

> I've had it up to here with some pious people who tell others who've found Christ and are in a second marriage, "You've got to go back to the first companion!" . . . that's not biblical and it's not logical.

> Deuteronomy 24 says you do not go back and try to live with the one you used to be with. The Lord meets us where we are. . . .

> Grace puts the past "under the blood." Grace says, "Start from here!" Take hold of the moment and, in Jesus Christ, live according to God's ideals from that point. (PP. 14–15)

Another restriction on remarriage is found in Leviticus 21:7—"They [the priests] shall not take a woman who is profaned by harlotry, nor shall they take a woman divorced from her husband; for he is holy to his God." This concept may have its New Testament counterpart in the qualification that an elder should be the husband of only one wife (1 Timothy 3:2). There are restrictions placed on the leaders of God's people that do not always apply to laypersons.

Jesus also forbids the remarriage of people who have divorced without just cause (Matthew 5:32; 19:9; Mark 10:11–12; Luke 16:18). Omitting the exception clause for the moment, let us examine Jesus' words restricting remarriage.

> I say to you that everyone who divorces his wife . . . makes her commit adultery; and whoever marries a divorced woman commits adultery (Matthew 5:32).

This passage has the woman's marriage in mind. The first husband is guilty of, in effect, forcing his ex-wife to commit adultery, and the other man who marries her is also guilty of adultery. This does not speak of the first man's remarriage or whether it would also be considered adultery. However, in a later statement, Jesus clears this up:

> I say to you, whoever divorces his wife . . . and marries another woman commits adultery (Matthew 18:8).

In Mark 10:11–12, Jesus teaches:

> Whoever divorces his wife and marries another woman commits adultery against her; and if she herself divorces her husband and marries another man, she is committing adultery.

In Luke 16:18, Jesus says,

> Everyone who divorces his wife and marries another commits adultery; and he who marries one who is divorced from a husband commits adultery.

Since Jesus cannot condone or promote adultery, the obvious conclusion is that apart from the exception clause he was forbidding the remarriage of divorced persons.

The Assemblies of God understands these passages (Matthew 5:32; 19:9; Mark 10:11–12; Luke 16:18) from a literal perspective. Thus, concerning the remarriage aspect, they interpret these statements of Jesus as condemning remarriage. Remarriage is seen "as an act of adultery, a sin against the covenant of the first marriage. . . . By doing so [remarrying] they would commit adultery and cause the new partner to commit adultery" (position paper, p. 12). And, according to the position paper, the purpose of Jesus' teaching on the adultery within remarriage was not simply to advance that particular bit of knowledge but was "to prevent [discourage] divorce in the first place" (p. 12).

The apostle Paul also gives restrictions on remarriage. He states that a Christian couple is not to divorce. However, if they disobey this command, which he attributes to the Lord, then they are to remain single, not remarry. This leaves open the opportunity for their reconciliation (1 Corinthians 7:10–11).

Sometimes Christian couples take these words of Paul to mean that if they do not have the same calling of God on their lives, they can leave one another: They have a "mixed-faith" marriage. Thus they believe they have the apostle's blessing to divorce so each of them can follow God's calling as each of them perceive it. And since they feel that they have the blessing of Scripture to divorce, they would also have the same blessing to remarry.

However, when Paul speaks about the unbeliever leaving, he is not speaking about the difference of the calling God has placed on individuals, but the difference in being a born-again believer and not being a born-again believer. This is fully realized when one looks at Paul's full treatment of the situation: 1 Corinthians 7:12–16. In verses 12–13 he speaks of the "unbelieving" wife and husband. No differences in the calling of God is mentioned, only the difference between the "brother" and a "wife who is an unbeliever." Then Paul sets up a contrast between the woman and her "unbelieving husband."

Paul goes on to say that "the unbelieving husband is sanctified through his wife and the unbelieving wife is sanctified through her believing husband" (1 Corinthians 7:14). If this mixed-faith marriage were simply one of calling and both husband and wife were truly born-again Christians, the husband would have no need to be sanctified through his wife. Nor would the wife need to be sanctified through her husband. The source of sanctification for the born-again person is Jesus Christ. One's sanctification is obtained through one's own faith in Christ. The great reformer Martin Luther, commenting on the subject of sanctification in his commentary on Galatians, said, "Whosoever then do believe in Christ, whether they be men or women, bond or free, etc., are all saints [sanctified]: not by their own works, but by the works of God, which they receive by faith."[1]

Admittedly much turmoil can develop between a husband and wife who feel God has given them different callings. But it is not within the scope of this study to give an answer to such a situation. In some cases it may call for the couple to seek pastoral or professional Christian counseling. Even so, divorce is not the answer: It is forbidden by both Jesus and Paul (Mark 10:11–12; 1 Corinthians 7:10). The Assemblies of God adheres to Paul's statement that married believers are not to divorce. If, however, the Christian couple does divorce, they are restricted from remarriage, unless of course they remarry each other.

As noted above, the Law, Jesus, and the apostle Paul have put restrictions on remarriage. Otherwise, remarriage is an acceptable option.

6

Remarriage: Exceptions

The Exception Clause

In the midst of Jesus' statements about husbands unlawfully divorcing their wives and causing them to commit adultery, and they themselves also committing adultery should they remarry, comes what is known as the exception clause: If a man divorces his wife he makes her commit adultery, unless (except) he divorces her because of "fornication" (Matthew 5:32).

Jesus covers many topics in His Sermon on the Mount (Matthew 5 through 7), one of which is divorce and remarriage. He says, "Anyone who divorces his wife, except for marital unfaithfulness, causes her to become an adulteress" (Matthew 5:32, NIV). When the wife is guilty of unfaithfulness, the divorcing of her by her husband does not make her commit adultery; she is already guilty of that. In that situation the man is then free from the marriage covenant, for it has been nullified by the actions of the wife.

It is important to note that Jesus was addressing marriage between believers. He was not dealing with the mixed-faith marriage here. He is also speaking to believers (see Matthew 5:1–2). And it is to them He states that there is one, and only one, legitimate reason for divorce: "fornication" (i.e., "marital unfaithfulness").

Matthew 19 also contains the exception clause: "Whoever divorces his wife, except for immorality [*porneia*, fornication], and marries another woman commits adultery" (Matthew 19:9). Regarding the historicity of this text the Assemblies of God position paper states:

> Some manuscripts omit "and marries another," but others, including the Sinaitic manuscript, contain it, and the sense of the context calls for it. There is no manuscript evidence for leaving out the exceptive clause. (P. 13)

Jay Adams concurs, bringing up the topic of the historicity of the exception clauses just long enough to defend them:

> There is no problem regarding the textual evidence for these clauses, and hardly anyone disputes their genuineness. (P. 52)

As has already been determined, the word "fornication" *(porneia)* in these passages is a term denoting a wide variety of sexual activity, including premarital, extramarital, homosexual, incestuous, and so on. However, the Assemblies of God maintains the position that this exception clause is not referring to a onetime act of illicit sexual behavior.

> In this verse the best manuscripts read: "Whosoever puts away [divorces] his wife except for fornication [habitual sexual immorality] and marries another, commits adultery."
>
> It should be emphasized that the exception has in view sexual immorality, not merely a single act. Wherever possible, sexually immoral practices should be dealt with through repentance, confession, forgiveness, and reconciliation, thus saving the marriage. (Position paper, p. 13)

Fornication *(porneia)* is used in Scripture to indicate an illicit relationship or life-style. Paul uses the word *(porneia)* in 1 Corinthians when he rebukes the Corinthian church for allowing fornication of the most appalling kind to go on in their midst without putting a stop to it (1 Corinthians 5:1–2). Jude speaks of the fornication of the wicked cities of Sodom, Gomorrah, and the surrounding cities. God destroyed those cities because of their continual fornication. John MacArthur also seems to confirm this idea in his teaching when he says,

> If a person committed adultery and then repented of it, he was to be forgiven and restored in love—Just as God will take back His adulterous wife, Israel, and as Hosea brought back his adulterous wife, Gomer. However, in the case of hard-hearted adultery in which a person would not turn and repent, divorce was an option—it was permitted. (PP. 53–54)

Some argue that these exception clauses should not be given heed because neither Mark nor Luke record them. However, rather than arguing for a position because something is not there, it seems much more logical and exegetical to argue for something that is there. Mark and Luke do not record the exception clause, yet Matthew records it twice. The historicity of the exception clauses is accepted, thus they are holy Scripture and demand attention, not rejection.

Extent of Exception Clauses

People giving serious attention to the exception clauses have asked: How far do these exception clauses extend? Do the exception clauses refer only to the divorce aspect of the passage, or do they refer to the remarriage aspect as well?

In Matthew 19:9, Jesus says if a man remarries after divorcing his wife (unless he divorced her for fornication) he commits adultery. The final outcome of the whole argument is the person's standing within the context of his new marriage. The custom of the people of Jesus' time was divorce *and* remarriage, just as it had been in Moses' time (Cosby, p. 90).

Remarriage was the rule, not the exception. So when Jesus answered the Pharisees' question, he naturally had in mind the milieu of his day. Therefore, when Jesus said that a divorce and *remarriage* without the cause of fornication were adulterous, the reverse must apply as well: Divorce due to fornication and subsequent remarriage is not adulterous.

In answering the question, Do the exception clauses extend to the remarriage as well as to the divorce? Jay Adams states:

> The answer is yes. There is no way of separating the two ideas in Matthew 19:9 or in Matthew 5:32. In the former passage, Jesus says that one commits adultery by marrying another unless he has divorced his previous wife for fornication. That is the whole point of the statement about adultery. Moreover, in the latter, the divorced wife and her second husband are warned that they will commit adultery unless she was divorced for fornication. (PP. 52–53)

Commenting on Matthew 19:9, the Assemblies of God position paper observes:

> Some, including those who follow the tradition of the Roman Catholics, say that the exceptive clause does not apply to "and married another, commits adultery." In this view, fornication or habitual sexual immorality, gives the right to separation from bed and board but does not sever the bond of marriage or give any right to dissolve it. But this is difficult to fit in with other passages which deal with the responsibilities of husband and wife (1 Corinthians 7:2–5). Therefore, most Protestants have always taken the position that the exceptive clause does apply to "and marries another."
>
> It should also be pointed out that in the extreme cases where divorce seems necessary, Jesus did not command

remarriage. However, it is clear that in Matthew 19:9 Jesus assumes the man will remarry. The verse deals with divorce *and* remarriage, and the laws of grammar make the exceptive clause apply to both. The Greek word for "put away" *(apoluo)* is used with regard to the Deuteronomy passage referred to in Matthew 5:31 and Mark 10:2–12. There, the "putting away" clearly did dissolve the marriage bond. Jesus did not change the nature of divorce as dissolving marriage. He simply threw out all excuses, reasons, or causes except "fornication" *(porneia,* habitual sexual immorality). However, in no case does He command divorce or remarriage. They are merely permitted under this one condition. (PP. 13–14)

Neither Romans 7:2–3 nor 1 Corinthians 7:39 makes any exception to the dissolution of marriage by death alone. Some people point this out as proof that no other reason exists for a marriage to be broken. However, one passage cannot be accepted to the exclusion of another. Death does indeed break the marriage covenant. Yet, the Assemblies of God also maintains that since Matthew 5:32 and 19:9 state that fornication dissolves the marriage, then fornication also breaks the marriage covenant. It need not be an either/or interpretation: *Both* death *and* fornication break the marriage covenant. Glen Cole is citing the latter when he answers the question of justification for remarriage: ". . . when one's mate is guilty of sexual immorality and is unwilling to repent and live faithfully with the marriage partner" (p. 18).

From the Assemblies of God perspective, the exception clauses plainly extend to remarriage. Therefore, when one divorces on the grounds of fornication (habitual sexual immorality), it is simply a recognition of the fact that the marriage covenant is already broken by the fornicator, and the innocent party has the legal and scriptural option to remarry.

Paul's Exception

Though Paul gives no exception for remarriage other than death in Romans 7:2–3 or 1 Corinthians 7:39, he does give an exception in 1 Corinthians 7:15. In this exception Paul is dealing with mixed-faith marriages: "If the unbelieving one leaves, let him leave; the brother or sister is not under bondage [not enslaved] in such cases, but God has called us to peace." Paul says that the remaining believer is "not under bondage in such cases." According to *Strong's Exhaustive Concordance,* bondage *(douloo)* means "to enslave—bring into (be under) bondage . . . to become (make) [a] servant."[1] Vine has it, *"Douloo . . .* signifies to make a slave of, to bring into bondage" (p. 131).

A brother or sister is not to be brought into bondage because of it. *Williams New Testament* reads: "If the unbelieving consort [literally, "unbeliever"] actually leaves, let the separation stand. In such cases the Christian husband or wife is *not morally bound;* God has called us to live in peace" (1 Corinthians 7:15, emphasis added).

This term "not under bondage" has definite implications for the innocent party. Those implications find their expression in answering the often asked questions: Is the person only free from an immoral spouse, or free to actually remarry?

As noted above, the term "bondage" *(douloo)* means to make one a slave. In Old Testament times among the Hebrews, a person who was in debt beyond his ability to pay could sell himself or hire out to servanthood *(doulos)* (Leviticus 25:39). However, a relative of the slave could redeem him from slavery at any time (Leviticus 25:48–49). If no one did, he would be set free by his master after six years (Deuteronomy 15:12–14). When a slave was set free, either by a relative's redemption payment or by serving the six years, he was a completely free man. In fact, he was freed from his previous master to the extent that he could voluntarily become the slave of a different master. He was no longer "under bondage" to his first master.

This is the same idea in Paul's words, "The brother or sister is not under bondage in such cases." Paul does not say the remaining believer is not free to remarry—as he does in verse 11 when speaking of Christians divorcing.

Cosby also sees the remaining brother or sister as free to remarry:

> Although Christians should not initiate divorce, Paul states that when the nonbeliever initiates [divorce], the believer is free from that relationship, and the indication is that he or she is free to remarry. (P. 131)

Likewise Dobson agrees that the remaining spouse is free to remarry. Dobson states that when the unbeliever has divorced the believer, "The saved person is not under obligation to the marriage covenant and is therefore free to remarry" (p. 78).

According to the Assemblies of God position paper, 1 Corinthians 7:15 includes an exception that opens the door for the innocent party to remarry. "The plain meaning seems to be that the believer is set free to remarry if he or she so chooses" (p. 16). Thus, the person who has been divorced by an unbelieving spouse is no longer bound by the marriage covenant and is free to remarry.

Divorce and Remarriage

Remarriage, however, is not always in the best interest of the divorcee. The Assemblies of God position paper points out: "Paul, however, does discourage remarriage for the sake of ministering unto the Lord" (p. 16). Specifically, Paul says,

> Are you bound to a wife? Do not seek to be released.

> Are you released from a wife? Do not seek a wife. . . . But I want you to be free from concern. One who is unmarried is concerned about the things of the Lord, how he may please the Lord; but one who is married is concerned about the things of the world, how he may please his wife, and his interests are divided (1 Corinthians 7:27, 32–34).

Though Paul does discourage remarriage he does not say that it is against the will of God. The word "released" is used twice in 1 Corinthians 7:27. But in each case, the two Greek words translated "released" are different: The first is *luo,* the second is *lusis. Luo,* according to *Strong's Exhaustive Concordance,* means "to 'loosen' (literally or figuratively): break (up), destroy, dissolve" and *lusis* means "a loosening, that is, (specifically) *divorce"* (p. 45). Vine concurs with Strong: "*Luo* denotes to loose, unbind, release . . . of the marriage tie, 1 Corinthians 7:27," and "*Lusis,* . . . 1 Corinthians 7:27, [speaks] of divorce" (pp. 887–888). Therefore, 1 Corinthians 7:27 can literally read: Are you married to a wife? Do not seek to *break up or dissolve* the marriage tie. Are you *divorced* from a wife? Do not seek a wife.

The first part of the next verse says, "But if you should marry, you have not sinned" (1 Corinthians 7:28). When verse 27 and 28 are read together it says: Are you married to a wife? Do not seek to *break up or dissolve* the marriage tie. Are you *divorced* from a wife? Do not seek a wife. But if you should remarry, you have not sinned.

It is quite clear from this passage of Scripture that remarriage—far from being the "unpardonable" sin—is no sin at all. Paul says, Are you divorced? Then don't go looking for a wife, *but if you do remarry, you have not sinned.*

That Paul is speaking to divorced persons here rather than just the people who have never been married needs to be established. The word *lusis* in verse 27 is not "unmarried" but "divorced." If it were "unmarried," the verse would say:

"Are you unmarried (never been married) from a wife?" The problem with this interpretation is obvious; this verse says "are you *released?*" One cannot be released from something or someone to which one was never bound. The word in the Greek is *lusis,* and both Strong and Vine translate it "divorce." One would have to arbitrarily give the word *lusis* another meaning to arrive at the idea that this passage is saying, "Have you never been married?"

Furthermore, Paul himself clears up the matter of whom he is addressing. After he says, "If you should marry, you have not sinned," he continues by saying, "if a virgin should marry, she has not sinned." Obviously a virgin is one who has never been married. Paul makes this distinction now because he had been addressing divorcees (the "released"): He has shifted his address to the unmarried (the "virgin"). Thus two different groups of people are represented in this passage: those who are released and those who were never bound, the divorced and the virgin.

Remarriage—A New Covenant

The issue has already been settled that if a person divorces on scriptural grounds and remarries, the new marriage is not an adulterous one. On the other hand, a person who gets a divorce and remarries but has no scriptural grounds for doing so is clearly committing an act of adultery (see Matthew 5:32, 19:9; Mark 10:11–12; Luke 16:18).

But what if an unbeliever has divorced and remarried without scriptural grounds and then wants to become a Christian—what is he or she to do, divorce the second spouse and return to the first, or stay in the new, second marriage? Some people teach that if one is divorced and remarried without proper scriptural justification, one is living in a state of continual adultery. To become right with God, that person must divorce the second spouse and remarry the original.

Those who advocate returning to the former spouse believe that since the second marriage was entered into unscripturally, it has been nothing more than a continuous state of adultery. According to Jesus, when one remarries after divorcing unlawfully, adultery definitely results. But is there such a thing as a state of adultery? Glen Cole answers:

> Nowhere does the Bible say that anyone lives in a continual state of adultery. Adultery is an act; it is not a continuing state.
>
> If a person is divorced and remarried [without the benefit of Scriptural grounds], the first act of sexual intercourse constitutes adultery in that marriage. That then establishes that marriage, and from then on, they're living as husband and wife. There is no such thing as a "state of adultery" in God's Word. It is an impossibility. It is an act. (P. 18)

The Assemblies of God position paper amplifies this interpretation. With the new marriage is the sin of adultery, and this is a sin against the previous marriage covenant. But at that point the first covenant is broken and the second one entered into. Since the first covenant is broken, the former partner is free to remarry. Since the second covenant has been entered into by law and scriptural grounds, it is incumbent upon the couple of the new marriage to be faithful to it. In fact, God expects the new covenant to be honored by all parties.

> Once a person remarries he is then obligated to be faithful to the new contract. . . . The Bible shows that God expects contracts to be kept even when entered into wrongly. When Joshua wrongly entered into a contract with the Gibeonites, God not only expected him to fulfill it, He gave him miracles of a hailstorm and the long day to help him (Joshua 9 and 10). Isaiah warned Ahaz against making a covenant with the Assyrians, but he

made it anyway (Isaiah 7). Then God warned Hezekiah
against breaking it and going down to Egypt for help
(Isaiah 30 and 31). (P. 17)

The new marriage is to be honored, and there is to be no
divorcing and returning to the former spouse. God recognizes
the new marriage as a lawful covenant, and the married
partners are to be faithful to that covenant.

7

Membership

The official statement on membership in the Assemblies of God is that it is "open to all born-again believers" (p. 18), including people who divorced and remarried before their conversion. They should not be placed under some ecclesiastical obligation to change their social or legal standing when they come to know the Lord. As a matter of fact, Paul told the Corinthian believers to hold steady: "Each one should remain in the situation which he was in when God called him" (1 Corinthians 7:20, NIV).

In the Corinthian church were mixed-marriages; it is possible that some of them were second marriages, with ex-spouses still living. Yet Paul tells the believers there that they are not to divorce the spouse who does not believe. It is pointed out that a great many divorces and remarriages were occurring in the Roman communities during the New Testament period, that the Gentiles in the household of Cornelius (Acts 10 to 11) were probably no exception, that most likely some of them had been improperly divorced and remarried—yet God accepted them (position paper, p. 18).

Speaking of the situation of being unscripturally divorced and remarried and then becoming born-again, Glen Cole says,

> What do you do with people like this but to help them start from that point and obey the Word of God!
>
> You can't go back and untangle the past. . . . when you break an egg, you cannot put it back together. Once it is scrambled, you cannot put it back.

> You must take these people from where they are. That's what God is saying to us in His Word. He that is in Christ is *new,* and goes from that point to serve the Lord.
>
> . . .
>
> The "new creature" attitude needs to prevail in the church of Jesus Christ. We must not squeeze out the possibilities of life-recovery in people who have had marital misfortunes before their conversion experience. God is a God of hope! There is *always* forgiveness! There is *always* deliverance in Him—*always!* (P. 14)

Membership is open to those who have had less than an ideal marriage in the past. The position paper makes the point succinctly: "If God accepts such believers, who are we to judge?" (position paper, p. 18).

That is not to say that the Assemblies of God is without restrictions on membership of people because of marital situations:

> In no case shall a person be accepted into membership while living in a common-law state of matrimony. (Position paper, p. 18)

Ministry Different from Membership

The question of whether a remarried person can be a deacon or pastor in the Assemblies of God is often asked. The requirements of ministry (pastor, deacon) are more restrictive than those of membership. Though a person who has been divorced and remarried may be accepted into membership in the Assemblies of God, he or she would not be eligible for certain ministerial positions.

In the Assemblies of God the basic restriction of such persons from the pastoral position comes from Paul's letter to Timothy. In 1 Timothy 3:2–7 the apostle Paul lists the qualifications for being an elder. He leads off with, "An overseer [pastor] . . . must be above reproach, the husband of one wife" (1 Timothy 3:2). In the same chapter he writes, "Let deacons be husbands of only one wife" (v. 12). Thus, the offices of pastor and deacon are not open to those who are remarried. These qualifications are not imposed on people for entrance into the Church as members of the body of Christ. God accepts any repentant person, no matter the entanglements of his past. Nevertheless, that same person may not be qualified for positions of leadership. God definitely has more stringent requirements for leadership than membership.

According to the two most popular interpretations of the phrase, "the husband of one wife," Paul was referring to either polygamy or remarriage. If the reference to more than one wife denotes polygamy only, then this passage does not apply to the person who has been divorced and remarried. However, the Assemblies of God position paper appeals to the history of the period: "Polygamy was not generally practiced" (p. 19).

As a matter of fact, according to Dobson, "Polygamy was prohibited by Roman law." Thus, he observes, "it would seem unnecessary that Paul would add this requirement [the exclusion of polygamists from eldership or deacon] if polygamy was already against the law" (p. 85).

Therefore, it is logical to assume that Paul was not speaking about polygamy, something virtually non-existent. Rather, he was speaking about divorce and remarriage, something obviously prevalent at this time as indicated by Jesus' addressing the subject (Matthew 5:32; 19:9) and Paul's answering the Corinthians about it (1 Corinthians 7).

The Assemblies of God maintains that the term "the husband of one wife" speaks to the problem of divorce and remarriage, not polygamy. Therefore, the remarried person is disqualified from the position of eldership (pastor) or deacon.

A further restriction concerning remarriage also applies.

Not only is a remarried person who has a former spouse living disqualified from ministry, but so too is the person who is married to someone who has a former living spouse. Therefore, if a man enters into his first marriage but his wife is divorced and her former spouse is living, then the man is disqualified for ministry in the Assemblies of God based upon his wife's divorce and remarriage. Thus, if either marriage partner has been divorced with a former spouse living, neither person can hold Assemblies of God ministerial credentials. Joseph R. Flower states:

> It would not be proper for any married persons to hold ministerial credentials with the General Council of the Assemblies of God if either marriage partner has a former living companion, unless they can qualify for an annulment of that former marriage according to the standard set by the Assemblies of God for such.[1]

At the same time it should be pointed out that the Assemblies of God makes a distinction between the divorcee and the remarried in ministry. An Assemblies of God minister who goes through divorce is not necessarily removed from leadership. Both the position of leadership and credentials may be retained providing the minister's district presbytery determines that the responsibility for the divorce does not lie with the minister. For example, Northwest District Superintendent Frank Cole states:

> An Assemblies of God minister who is divorced may remain in the Assemblies of God as a minister with credentials as long as he or she does not marry. Also, a person who is not an Assemblies of God minister and who is divorced though not remarried may obtain credentials as an Assemblies of God minister.
>
> Divorced and not remarried persons are taken into consideration independently on the merit of each in-

dividual's situation. Their circumstances surrounding the divorce would have a bearing on the situation.[2]

The determining factor of the minister's position of leadership is not necessarily divorce, but remarriage. For Paul says that the elder (pastor) is to be the husband of only one wife (1 Timothy 3:2). A divorced minister may therefore continue in ministry as long as he or she remains unmarried and thereby continues to fulfill the limited one spouse requirement. And indeed, the Assemblies of God has ministers (pastors, evangelists) who have gone through divorce and have not been required to relinquish their credentials nor resign their position of leadership.

Higher qualifications for leadership than for membership are not peculiar to the New Testament. In the Old Testament, God placed greater restrictions on those Israelites who were to be priests than on those who were not. As was pointed out in the last chapter, among the restrictions for Levitical priests was, "They shall not take a woman who is profaned by harlotry, nor shall they take a woman divorced from her husband" (Leviticus 21:7). Yet it is also very clear that for the ordinary Israelite, marrying a divorced woman presented no problem (Deuteronomy 24:1–4).

Not everyone is called to a position of leadership, and not everyone is qualified for leadership. The Assemblies of God position paper states:

> We must remember that the Bible does not indicate that everyone is to have a turn at these offices in the church. The Bible lays down specific requirements for elders and deacons. The requirement that they be the husband of one wife is in keeping with the requirement that they must have a good report from outside the church. Both for the sake of the witness of the church and for the sake of freedom from entanglements, those who administer the affairs of the local church must meet these and other qualifications. This in no way

> promotes a double standard of morality, but is simply
> a matter of qualifications for the specific ministries of
> elders and deacons. (P. 19)

There are positions of ministry and leadership that the remarried may fill in the church. Within the Assemblies of God, however, these ministries have not been formally identified. Glen Cole, speaking of the position of the Assemblies of God on this matter, states:

> The position of our movement has been that a divorced
> and remarried person whose former companion is still
> living cannot serve as a pastor or deacon. In most places,
> they can serve as a Sunday school teacher, a choir member, an usher, a cell leader or anything else.[3]

The Assemblies of God position paper states that though some would restrict remarried persons from *all* forms of leadership within the church, this is not biblical. "Every member of the Body has a function, and the ministries are given by the Spirit (1 Corinthians 12:11; Romans 12:6–8; Ephesians 4:16)" (p. 19).

Therefore, though a remarried person cannot become a minister in the Assemblies of God or hold a position as pastor or deacon, that person can serve in various other ministries within the church.

Appendix B contains the official position paper of the Assemblies of God on "Divorce and Remarriage." See pages 79–82 concerning the application of these biblical principles that have been discussed throughout this study. Under Article VII, Section 5c, there is a statement about the subject of annulments, and commentary will resume once again with that subject in the next chapter.

8

Annulments

The rule that a person who has been divorced and remarried or is married to a person who is divorced and has a living ex-spouse cannot be an elder (pastor) or deacon in the Assemblies of God has one exception: annulment. However, simply having a recognized annulment from the state does not secure one the scriptural position of a "God-approved" divorce. In a reexamination of its disapproval of divorced and remarried persons holding ministerial credentials, the Assemblies of God reiterated Article VII, section 5c, of its Bylaws:

> "We disapprove of any married persons holding ministerial credentials with the Assemblies of God or district councils granting credentials to such, if either marriage partner has a former companion living," the only exception being if a former marriage is annulled *in the view of the [General Council] Executive Presbytery.*[1]

The Executive Presbytery of the Assemblies of God retains the right to judge whether a person's annulment by the state (lawful but not ecclesiastical) is in fact based on "clear and satisfactory evidence of an illegal marriage through deception or fraud" (position paper, p. 23). If the state-granted annulment is found lacking, the Assemblies of God further retains the authority to exclude the person with the annulment from holding ministerial credentials with the denomination. As Jay Adams has observed, "The state never was competent to judge grounds for divorce. (Neither the state nor lawyers can do exegesis)" (p. 47).

At the same time, the Assemblies of God also retains the authority to judge whether a person's state-granted "divorce or dissolution" would be better designated an annulment. If the Executive Presbytery determines that a divorce is more appropriately deemed an annulment, the person will not be excluded from holding ministerial credentials with the Assemblies of God based solely on his or her divorce and remarriage.

Obtaining an ecclesiastical annulment, however, is not easy. For what must be proved is the illegality of the marriage, that the offending spouse entered into the marriage by fraud or with the intent to deceive.

The first step in seeking the annulment is to write one's district superintendent, giving all pertinent information regarding the divorce. If one has information in the form of letters, for example, it is good to send photocopies. If the district office believes enough evidence to pursue an annulment has been presented, an application for annulment will be sent to the inquirer. Once the application is fully completed with all pertinent information and is sent to the District Executive Presbytery, they will review it.

The District Executive Presbytery has it within its power to accept or reject the application for annulment, as the members deem appropriate. If the material does not prove that there was fraud or deception on the part of the spouse, then it does not warrant further consideration. Thus, the District Executive Presbytery will inform the person that the annulment is denied.

If, however, the material does warrant further consideration, the district office will send the materials with its recommendation for annulment to the General Council Executive Presbytery. If that body grants the annulment, it will inform the district office and the district office will in turn inform the individual. If, however, the General Council Executive Presbytery denies the annulment, the individual may appeal the decision.

The appeal of the General Council Executive Presbytery's decision is made to the General Council General Presbytery. However, it will review the appeal only if there is additional pertinent material for consideration, material that the General Council Executive Presbytery did not have in the course of its evaluation.

Anyone who attempts this route of annulment should be fully aware that it is very difficult to prove that the marriage was entered into through fraud or deception by the spouse. As well as reliving some painful circumstances, one may finally have one's hopes of annulment denied. For example, no matter the details surrounding the spouse's *leaving* the marriage, the basis for granting an annulment is the intent of the spouse when he or she *entered* into the marriage. Was there fraud or the intent to deceive at the time of the marriage? Can that be proven? If the answer to the last two questions is yes, then there is the possibility of annulment.

See Appendix A for a reproduction of an application for annulment.

9

Summary

What follows is a review of the main points of this study.

Marriage is not a human invention or institution. Marriage originated in the mind of God. "So God created man in his own image, in the image of God created he him; male and female created he them" (Genesis 1:27).

It is clear from Scripture that God's ideal for marriage is that of one man for one woman for life; marriage may only (ideally) be dissolved by death (Romans 7:2–3).

Marriage is a solemn, binding covenant made before God and man.

God hates divorce. One reason for God's loathing divorce is the pain for everyone involved.

"What therefore God has joined together, let no man separate" (Matthew 19:6). His command "let no man separate" what God has joined together is binding today.

God gave laws regulating divorce in an effort to put restrictions on mankind's wrong practices.

Moses never commanded divorce; it was only permitted and that because of the hardness of men's hearts.

Speaking to Christian couples Paul says that there is to be no divorce (1 Corinthians 7:10–11).

Paul says that a Christian is not to initiate a divorce in a mixed-faith marriage.

Jesus permitted a Christian to initiate a divorce when the spouse had committed fornication (habitual sexual immorality).

Remarriage is permitted after divorce if (1) the offending

spouse was guilty of fornication (habitual sexual immorality) or (2) the unbelieving spouse divorced the believer.

If a Christian couple do divorce against God's will and biblical command, they are to remain single, not remarrying, leaving open the possibility of reconciliation (1 Corinthians 7:10–11).

From the Assemblies of God perspective, there is no doubt that the exception clauses (permitting divorce because of fornication or the unbeliever's leaving) extend to remarriage.

Remarriage is a new covenant and is to be honored, and there is to be no divorcing and returning to the former spouse. God recognizes the new marriage as a lawful covenant and the married partners are to be faithful to that covenant.

Membership in the Assemblies of God is open to all born-again believers. This includes people who are divorced and remarried.

Persons living in a common-law marriage shall not be accepted into membership in the Assemblies of God.

God has more stringent requirements for leadership than membership.

The offices of elder (pastor) and deacon are closed to those who are remarried (1 Timothy 3:12).

A remarried person can serve in various other ministries within the church.

The Assemblies of God retains the right to deny credentials to a person with a state-granted annulment if, in their judgment, the annulment is lacking "clear and satisfactory evidence of an illegal marriage through deception or fraud."

The Assemblies of God may judge a person's state-granted divorce or dissolution to be better designated an annulment.

The obtaining of an ecclesiastical annulment is not easy.

The main principle that has to be proven to gain an annulment is that there was fraud or the intent to deceive on the part of the spouse *at the time the marriage was entered into.*

Appendix A

INSTRUCTIONS TO APPLICANT

1. *Please read application before beginning to fill in information.*

2. *Use typewriter only.*

3. *In order to enable the Executive Presbytery to render a just decision, and in view of its limited time in session, it is mandatory that all questions be fully answered and all requested information supplied herewith. Failure to do so will result in return of the application.*

A. Your name _____

Street address _____

City_____State _____Zip _____

Age_____

B. 1. Do you have credentials now?_____

2. What credentials?_____

3. With what district or organization? _____

4. In what ministry are you presently engaged? _____

5. If a pastor, state church? _____

C. PRESENT MARRIAGE

1. How many times have you been married?_____

2. Are you presently married? _____

3. To whom? _____

4. Date and place of ceremony? _____

   _____

5. Your age at time of present marriage?_____

6. Present spouse's age at time of marriage? _____

7. Are you living with this spouse now? _____

D. PREVIOUS MARRIAGE

1. Were you married to another spouse previous to this marriage? _____

2. Name of previous spouse?_____

3. Date and place of ceremony? _____

4. Your age at date of marriage? _____

5. Spouse's age at date of marriage? _____

6. Minimum age requirement of state at time of marriage? _____

7. If either party to marriage was under age, how was the license obtained?

   _____

Form No. 737 007
Revised: 4-8-89

8. State length of courtship with first spouse? _____

9. Was the marriage consummated?_____ If answer is "no," state reason. _____

_____

_____

10. How long after marriage ceremony did you separate? _____

Date _____

11. Did you live together again after separation? _____

12. When did you last see your former spouse? _____

E. 1. Did your previous marriage end in: Annulment?_____ Divorce?_____

Dissolution?_____

2. Place: City _____ County_____ State _____

3. Who petitioned the court for termination of marriage, you or your spouse?

_____

4. Date of petition? _____

5. Name and location of court? _____

_____

6. *Attach hereto a copy of petition.*

7. State decree of termination granted by the court? _____

_____

_____

8. On what date granted? _____

9. Was a property settlement decreed by the court? _____

_____

_____

_____

10. Was alimony ordered by the court? _____

11. Were children born to the first union?_____ State how many and dates of

births. _____

_____

_____

12. *Attach copy of the court's decree dissolving the marriage.*

F. 1. Why did you petition for the termination of the marriage?_____

_____

_____

_____

_____

_____

_____

(If additional space is needed attach typewritten sheet)

2. What cause did you state during the proceedings in court?_____

_____

_____

_____

_____

3. If spouse petitioned for termination of marriage, what reasons were given there-
for? _____

_____

_____

_____

_____

G. 1. Prior to petitioning for the termination of the marriage, did you seek counsel or
advice?_____

From whom?_____

_____

_____

2. Please attach any letters which will corroborate your statement to us as to reason
why marriage could not continue.

3. It is expected that you will make an effort to obtain evidence from your former companion in corroboration of the information on your application. Please attach
documentation.

H. What is your purpose in placing this petition before the Executive Presbytery.

_____

_____

_____

I. When all questions have been answered and the requested documents attached, send
this application to the district council office, which will forward the same to the office
of the general secretary of the Assemblies of God.

_____

Applicant's signature

Date_____

Appendix B

Divorce and Remarriage

Application of Biblical Principles

A. *Marriage*

1. **Marriage is a basic human relationship.**

    a. Marriage is God-ordained. "God created man in his own image, in the image of God created he him; male and female created he them" (Genesis 1:27). The very nature of the way God created man to live on the earth indicates He intended man and woman for each other.

    Their relationship was to be social as well as physical. "The Lord God said, It is not good that the man should be alone; I will make him a help meet for him" (Genesis 2:18).

    The first woman was a "help meet" (a counterpart) for the man, taken from his side, bone of his bones and flesh of his flesh, his perfect complement (Genesis 2:23). It is obvious that God meant them

    to share in both privilege and responsi-
bility.

b. God intended marriage to be a lifelong
monogamous union. "Therefore shall a
man leave his father and his mother, and
shall cleave [stay joined in love and loy-
alty] unto his wife: and they shall be one
flesh" (Genesis 2:24). When this is quoted
in Matthew 19:5 a Greek word for *cleave*
is used which means "to be glued to, be
closely bound to."

The Old Testament factually recognized
that polygamy did exist. It notes that the
first case of polygamy was in Cain's line
(Genesis 4:19) and shows that monogamy was still the ideal (Psalm 128:3;
Proverbs 5:18; 31:10-29; Ecclesiastes 9:9).
Jesus also acknowledges that God's ideal
in the beginning was monogamy (Matthew 19:8).

2. **Marriage involves a covenant.**

Marriage is a covenant, a solemn binding
agreement made before God and man. "The
Lord hath been witness between thee and
the wife of thy youth, against whom thou
hast dealt treacherously: yet is she thy companion, and the wife of thy *covenant*" (Malachi 2:14, emphasis added).

Ezekiel applies the idea of marriage to the
relationship between God and Israel. "Yea,
I sware unto thee, and entered into a *cov-*

6

enant with thee, saith the Lord God, and thou becamest mine" (Ezekiel 16:8, emphasis added). From what is said we see that the husband "sware unto" the wife (took an oath, pledged faith) and entered into a solemn covenant not intended to be broken. The Hebrew word used, however, implies no sacrifice, thereby distinguishing it from the word used for the more sacred and binding "cut a covenant." The love involved is fundamentally the Hebrew *hesed,* "a loyal, covenant keeping love," which God shows us even when we are unworthy.

B. *Divorce*
  1. **God hates divorce.**
    a. "The Lord hath been witness between thee and the wife of thy youth, against whom thou hast dealt treacherously: yet is she thy companion, and the wife of thy covenant. And did not he make one? Yet had he the residue of the Spirit. And wherefore one? That he might seek a godly seed. Therefore take heed to your spirit, and let none deal treacherously against the wife of his youth. For the Lord, the God of Israel, saith that he hateth putting away: for one covereth violence with his garment, saith the Lord of hosts: therefore take heed to your spirit, that ye deal not treacherously" (Malachi 2:14-16).

7

This passage shows that divorce is treachery (deceitful unfaithfulness) against your companion. It is also a violent thing coming from a wrong spirit. Worst of all, it hinders the growth of a "godly seed." Broken homes do not tend to produce the healthiest offspring.

b. "What therefore God hath joined [yoked] together, let not man put asunder" (Matthew 19:6). Divorce was not in God's original intention for man. God's purposes in marriage are not helped by breaking the yoke. They can only be carried out as the pair subject themselves to Christ and each other. Such a relationship is beautifully described in Ephesians 5:21-31.

2. **The Law restricted divorce.**

The Law recognized the fact that divorce was taking place in Israel (as were many other practices common to the ancient world). In giving Israel the Law, God accepted people where they were, put restrictions on their wrong practices, and tried to direct them.

In their confrontation with Jesus about divorce, the Pharisees were obviously in error when they said Moses *commanded* that a man give a certificate of divorce when putting his wife away (divorcing her). Jesus said that Moses only "suffered," or permitted,

8

them to do so—and then not for "every cause," as was commonly practiced at that time (Matthew 19:3,7,8).

This is borne out in Deuteronomy 24:1-4. The Hebrew Moses used there is a simple sequence that does not command divorce. He simply recognizes that men were divorcing their wives. The passage literally says that when a man divorces his wife "because he has found in her an unclean matter [a Hebrew word connected with uncovered stools (Deuteronomy 23:12-14), with Noah's nakedness (Genesis 9:21-23), and with Edom under the figure of a drunken woman (Lamentations 4:21)—that is, some moral or sexual uncleanness apart from adultery, since adultery would call for her death under the Law] and has written for her a certificate of divorce and given it into her hand and sent her away from his house, and she goes out of his house and has another husband [it is assumed she would do this] and the other husband hates her and writes her a certificate of divorce and gives it into her hand and sends her out of his house, or if the other husband dies who took her to be his wife, her first husband who sent her away shall not be able to return and take her (again) to be his wife."

In other words, a man is to think twice before he divorces his wife even for what seems to be a good reason. He might want her

9

back, but if she has married again, he could
not have her.

3. **Jesus forbade divorce as contrary to God's
will and word.**
He made this clear in Matthew 19:5,6 and
Mark 10:6-9.

4. **Paul forbade a Christian couple getting a
divorce.**
"Unto the married I command, yet not I,
but the Lord [Paul had an actual saying of
Jesus to back this up], Let not the wife depart from her husband: but and if she depart, let her remain unmarried, or be rec-
onciled to her husband: and let not the
husband put away his wife" (1 Corinthians
7:10,11).

Although Paul recognized that Christians
were getting divorces he commanded that
they keep the way open for reconciliation.

5. **Paul forbade Christians taking the initia-
tive in getting a divorce because their partner is an unbeliever.**
"But to the rest speak I, not the Lord [Paul
did not have an actual saying of Jesus to
back this up, though Paul was speaking under the inspiration of the Spirit]: If any
brother hath a wife that believeth not, and
she be pleased to dwell with him [as a faithful wife], let him not put her away. And the
woman which hath a husband that believeth
not, and if he be pleased to dwell with

10

her, let her not leave him. . . . But if the unbelieving depart, let him depart. A brother or a sister is *not under bondage [not enslaved]* in such cases" (1 Corinthians 7:12-15, emphasis added).

Thus Paul indicates that the Christian cannot stop an unbelieving partner from leaving (getting a divorce) if he or she insists on it.

6. **Jesus permitted a Christian to initiate a divorce when fornication was involved.**

"Whosoever shall put away his wife, saving for the cause of fornication, causeth her to commit adultery: and whosoever shall marry her that is divorced committeth adultery" (Matthew 5:32. See also Matthew 19:9). This is permission, however, not a command.

The Greek word for "fornication" *(porneia)* may include especially repeated acts of adultery, but usually means habitual sexual immorality of any kind, both before and after marriage. (A *porne* was a prostitute.) A few scholars would limit the meaning of fornication here to incest, but this is not the normal usage of the word.

Some would rule out this exception because it is not found in Mark and Luke, not wanting to build a teaching on just the two passages in Matthew. However, we accept the length of the millennium as spanning one thousand years even though this time period is mentioned in only one Bible passage

11

(Revelation 20:2-7). The same principle applies to other Bible teachings.

It is seldom, if ever, that any single passage gives all aspects of truth on any single theme. In order to come to an understanding of any truth, we must take the whole of what the Bible teaches.

C. *Remarriage*

1. **The Law accepted the fact that divorce permitted remarriage.**

   This is clear from the passage in Deuteronomy 24:1-4 already quoted. The same passage shows that the Law put some limits on remarriage. Malachi 2:11 condemned remarriage to an unbeliever. A priest was forbidden to take a divorced woman as his wife (Leviticus 21:7).

2. **Jesus in His basic teaching forbade the remarriage of divorced persons.**

   He condemned remarriage as an act of adultery, a sin against the covenant of the first marriage (Mark 10:11,12; Luke 16:18; Matthew 5:32; 19:9).

   However, Jesus recognized that the basic problem is divorce itself, for He saw that the divorced could be expected to remarry. By doing so they would commit adultery and cause the new partner to commit adultery. Thus, the basic purpose in what Jesus said is to prevent divorce in the first place.

3. **Matthew 5:32 added an exceptive clause.**
   "Whosoever shall put away his wife, saving for the cause of fornication [habitual sexual immorality] causeth her to commit adultery." This shows that a husband who divorces a sexually immoral woman does not cause her to commit adultery, since she is already guilty of adultery.

4. **Matthew 19:9 also carried this exceptive clause.**
   In this verse the best manuscripts read: "Whosoever puts away [divorces] his wife except for fornication [habitual sexual immorality] and marries another, commits adultery."*

   It should be emphasized that the exception has in view sexual immorality, not merely a single act. Wherever possible, sexually immoral practices should be dealt with through repentance, confession, forgiveness, and reconciliation, thus saving the marriage.

   Some, including those who follow the traditions of the Roman Catholics, say that the

---

*Some manuscripts omit "and marries another," but others, including the Sinaitic manuscript, contain it, and the sense of the context calls for it. There is no manuscript evidence for leaving out the exceptive clause. (See John Murray, *Divorce*, p. 40.)

13

exceptive clause does not apply to "and marries another, commits adultery." In this view, fornication, or habitual sexual immorality, gives the right to separation from bed and board but does not sever the bond of marriage or give any right to dissolve it. But this is difficult to fit in with other passages that deal with the responsibilities of husband and wife (1 Corinthians 7:2-5). Therefore, most Protestants have always taken the position that the exceptive clause does apply to "and marries another."

It should also be pointed out that in the extreme cases where divorce seems necessary, Jesus did not command remarriage. However, it is clear that in Matthew 19:9 Jesus assumes the man will remarry. The verse deals with divorce *and* remarriage, and the laws of grammar make the exceptive clause apply to both. The Greek word for "put away" *(apoluo)* is used with regard to the Deuteronomy passage referred to in Matthew 5:31 and Mark 10:2-12. There, the "putting away" clearly did dissolve the marriage bond. Jesus did not change the nature of divorce as dissolving marriage. He simply threw out all excuses, reasons, or causes except "fornication" *(porneia,* habitual sexual immorality). However, in no case does He command divorce or remarriage. They are merely permitted under this one condition.

14

Again, the objection is made that Romans 7:1-3 and 1 Corinthians 7:39 make no exception to the statement that marriage is dissolved by death. Thus some take this to mean that marriage is broken by death alone.

But these passages are stating basic principles and do not deal with the exceptions. Romans 7 recognizes that the husband under the Law could get a divorce, but the wife could not. Therefore, the wife was bound by "the law of her husband" until his death. We must also keep in mind that under the Law the penalty for adultery was death. This penalty of death was given not to break the marriage relationship, but in recognition that it was already broken.

5. **1 Corinthians 7:15 also contains an exception.**
   "If the unbelieving depart, let him depart. A brother or a sister is not under bondage [not enslaved] in such cases: but God hath called us to peace."

   "Not enslaved" is a strong expression. Yet some, insisting on the basis of Romans 7:2 that death alone can dissolve a marriage, interpret this passage to mean that the Christian is free to let the unbelieving partner go, but not free to remarry. However, we must remember that in Romans 7:2 Paul is not addressing the subject of divorce and remarriage. He is simply using the unique

15

situation of the woman under the Law in which only death could loose her from her husband to illustrate believers' complete dependence upon Christ's vicarious death to loose them from the claims of the Law. Paul was aware that under the Law the husband had the option of divorcing his wife (Deuteronomy 24:1-4), which was not available to the wife. Only death could loose her from the law of her husband. Sound principles of exegesis will not permit one to assume that Paul's view on the subject of divorce and remarriage appear here.

If a believer is "not enslaved" when an unbelieving spouse, unwilling to remain in the marriage, divorces him (or her), he (or she) must be considered set free. Since it is the unbelieving partner who determines to go and initiates a divorce, the believer's freedom seems to be more than a freedom to let him (or her) go, since he (or she) is going anyway. The plain meaning seems to be that the believer is set free to remarry if he or she so chooses.

Paul, however, does discourage remarriage for the sake of ministering to the Lord. "Are you free from a wife? Do not seek marriage. But if you marry, you do not sin" (1 Corinthians 7:27,28).

6. **Remarriage is a new contract or covenant.** Some say that a person who remarries is living in adultery. They say that though

16

adultery is not an unforgivable sin, true repentance will demand quitting the sin, as the thief must quit stealing. They argue that for a person who has remarried to live with the new partner involves them continually in acts of adultery. But to assume an analogy between marriage and thievery is erroneous. It is obvious that marriage always involves a contract, but thievery does not.

A remarriage entered into wrongly does indeed constitute an act of adultery against the previous contract. This breaks the old contract; the former partner is set free. Once a person remarries he is then obligated to be faithful to the new contract. Deuteronomy 24:4 showed it to be wrong to go back to the old marriage contract. (Hosea was later commanded to do so as an illustration of the love of God that would take back apostate Israel.)

The Bible shows that God expects contracts to be kept even when entered into wrongly. When Joshua wrongly entered into a contract with the Gibeonites, God not only expected him to fulfill it, He gave him miracles of a hailstorm and the long day to help him (Joshua 9 and 10). Isaiah warned Ahaz against making a covenant with the Assyrians, but he made it anyway (Isaiah 7). Then God warned Hezekiah against breaking it and going down to Egypt for help (Isaiah 30 and 31).

17

D. *The place of the divorced and remarried in the church*

1. **Membership is open to all born-again believers.**

   This would certainly include those who were divorced and remarried before they were saved. Paul indicates that those in various social and legal positions, such as the circumcised and those who were slaves, should be accepted in the condition in which they were when they were saved (1 Corinthians 7:17-24). "Brethren, let every man, wherein he is called, therein abide with God" (1 Corinthians 7:24).

   God accepted the Gentiles at the house of Cornelius (Acts 10 and 11). Knowing the frequency of divorce and remarriage among the Romans of the time, it is very probable that some at the house of Cornelius were so involved.

   Paul gives the Christian no option but to continue to live with the unbelieving partner who is willing to live with him or her. Again, it is very probable that many of these Corinthian believers were married to unbelievers who had previous spouses still living. If God accepts such believers, who are we to judge? However, in no case shall a person be accepted into membership while living in a common-law state of matrimony.

18

2. **The offices of elder and deacon are not open to those who are remarried.**

   The offices of elder (corresponding to pastor) and deacon are restricted by the requirement that they shall be "the husband of one wife" (1 Timothy 3:2,12). Some say this refers to polygamy. History clearly indicates, however, that polygamy was not generally practiced at the time, while divorce and remarriage were extremely common among both Gentiles and Jews.

   We must remember that the Bible does not indicate that everyone is to have a turn at these offices in the church. The Bible lays down specific requirements for elders and deacons. The requirement that they be the husband of one wife is in keeping with the requirement that they must have a good report from outside the church. Both for the sake of the witness of the church and for the sake of freedom from entanglements, those who administer the affairs of the local church must meet these and other qualifications. This in no way promotes a double standard of morality, but is simply a matter of qualifications for the specific ministries of elders and deacons.

   Some would restrict the remarried from all the ministries of the Church. However, every member of the Body has a function, and the ministries are given by the Spirit (1 Corinthians 12:11; Romans 12:6-8; Ephesians 4:16).

19

Application of Biblical Principles to Our Bylaws as Revised and Adopted by the General Council in Session

Article VIII, Section 5

Membership

(1) There are now among Christian people those who became entangled in their marriage relations in their former lives of sin and who do not see how these matters can be adjusted. We recommend that these people be received into the membership of local assemblies and that their marriage complications be left in the hands of the Lord (1 Corinthians 7:17,20,24).

(2) We recommend that in no case shall persons be accepted into membership who are known to be living in a common-law state of matrimony.

Remarriage

Low standards on marriage and divorce are very hurtful to individuals, to the family, and to the cause of Christ. Therefore, we discourage divorce by all lawful means and teaching. We positively disapprove of Christians getting divorces for any cause except fornication and adultery (Matthew 19:9). Where these exceptional circumstances exist or when a Christian has been divorced by an unbeliever, we recommend that the question of remarriage be resolved by the believer as he walks in the light of God's Word (1 Corinthians 7:15,27,28).

20

Local Church Leadership

(1) Since the New Testament restricts divorced and remarried believers from the church offices of bishop or elder and deacon, we recommend that this standard be upheld by all our assemblies (Titus 1:5-9; 1 Timothy 3:12). However, we recommend that all other opportunities for Christian service for which these believers may be qualified be made available to them.

(2) It is understood that recommendations are not binding, but local assemblies shall maintain the prerogative of setting their own standards (in accord with provisions of Article XI of the Constitution).

Performing Marriage Ceremonies

(1) We disapprove of any Assemblies of God minister performing a marriage ceremony for anyone who has been divorced and whose former companion is still living unless his case is included in the exceptional circumstances described in Article VIII, Section 5, paragraph *b.* Any minister of our fellowship who performs a ceremony for a disapproved marriage (indicated above), unless he has been innocently deceived into doing so, may be dismissed from the Fellowship. Assemblies of God ministers are required to counsel applicants for marriage ceremonies with scriptural guidelines for Christian marriage prior to the performing of the ceremony. They may not perform cere-

21

monies for persons who, in the minister's opinion, approach marriage without proper forethought, wisdom, and sobriety.

(2) We realize that the remarrying of such persons included in the exceptive circumstances in Article VIII, Section 5, paragraph *b*, could violate the conscience of a minister, and if this should be the case, the minister should not be expected to perform such ceremonies.

Ministerial Credentials

We disapprove of any married minister of the Assemblies of God holding credentials if either minister or spouse has a former companion living. (See, also, Article VII, Section 5, paragraphs *b* and *c*.)

Article VII, Section 5

a. It is recommended that our District Councils refrain from ordaining to the ministry any preacher who may have been licensed in another district until such licentiate shall have resided in the district in which he is seeking ordination at least one year and shall have met the requirements of the district granting him license, and until endorsement be secured from the officiary of the district in which the candidate was previously licensed.

b. We disapprove of District Councils granting credentials to married persons in cases where either the applicant or the married partner has a former companion living (See Article VIII, Section 5e).

c. The Executive Presbytery shall have the authority to determine whether an applicant's annulment of a former marriage is consistent with the scriptural position of the Fellowship relating to the granting or holding of ministerial credentials; or in the case of a divorce or a dissolution, whether the circumstances would more appropriately be classified as calling for an annulment. The application must be accompanied by clear and satisfactory evidence of an illegal marriage through deception or fraud. Appeals from the decision of the Executive Presbytery may be made to the General Presbytery.

Notes

Chapter 1. Marriage

[1]"Divorce and Remarriage," position paper, approved August 1973 (Springfield, Mo.: Gospel Publishing House, 1987), 5. Original page numbers for the position paper in Appendix B have been retained for reference purposes. Subsequent references to the position paper are also from this source.

[2]Jay E. Adams, *Marriage, Divorce, and Remarriage* (Grand Rapids: Baker Book House, 1980), 5. Subsequent references to Jay E. Adams are also from this source.

[3]William E. Pickthorn, ed., *Minister's Manual,* vol. 2, "Services for Weddings and Funerals" (Springfield, Mo.: Gospel Publishing House, 1965), 7. This particular ceremony bears witness to the traditional aspect of marriage, identified as "an old ceremony handed down in the family of the minister who originated it" (p. 10).

[4]Dwight Hervey Small, *The Right to Remarry* (Old Tappan, N.J.: Fleming H. Revell Company, 1977), 29–30. Subsequent references to Dwight Hervey Small are also from this source.

[5]W. E. Vine, Merrill F. Unger, William White, Jr., *An Expository Dictionary of Biblical Words* (Nashville: Thomas Nelson Publishers, 1984), 61. Subsequent references to W. E. Vine are also from this source.

[6]Fred H. Wight, *Manners and Customs of Bible Lands* (Chicago: Moody Press, 1953), 124. Subsequent references to Fred H. Wight are also from this source.

[7]Michael R. Cosby, *Sex in the Bible* (Englewood Cliffs, N.J.: Prentice Hall, Inc., 1984), 13. Subsequent references to Michael R. Cosby are also from this source.

[8]L. I. Granberg, "Theology of Marriage" in *Evangelical Dictionary of Theology,* Walter A. Elwell, ed. (Grand Rapids: Baker Book House, 1984), 694.

[9]One might argue that the position of *anti* homosexual marriages is assumed within the Assemblies of God and need not be brought up in a study of this kind. However, the question of homosexual marriages is given treatment here because of its growing acceptance and tolerance in American society in this day.

[10] Frank Cole, Northwest district superintendent of the Assemblies of God, letter to author, 18 November 1987.

[11]Edward G. Dobson, *What the Bible Really Says About Marriage, Divorce and Remarriage* (Old Tappan, N.J.: Fleming H. Revell Company, 1988), 18. Subsequent references to Edward G. Dobson are also from this source.

Chapter 2. Divorce

[1]Richard Dobbins, "Divorce: Permitted But Not Prescribed," *Charisma,* March 1978, 12. There does not seem to be an explicit passage that confirms this statement. However, Dobbins uses Malachi 2:16 as his starting point. Malachi 2:14–15 mentions the hurt wife and the offspring. Subsequent references to Richard Dobbins are also from this source.

[2]A. B. Bonds, Jr., as quoted from "Christian Victory" in "Scars of Divorce" *Pentecostal Evangel,* 2 December 1962, 16.

[3]"More Divorces, Deaths, and Births, Fewer Marriages in U.S. in 1985, Preliminary Figures Show," *Pentecostal Evangel,* 25 May 1986, 24.

Chapter 3. Paul on Divorce

[1]Leon Morris, *The First Epistle of Paul to the Corinthians,* vol. 7, Tyndale New Testament Commentaries (Grand Rapids: Wm. B. Eerdmans, 1981), 109; see also C. K. Barrett, *The First Epistle to the Corinthians,* Harper's New Testament Commentaries (New York: Harper & Row, 1968), 163. Subsequent references to C. K. Barrett are also from this source.

[2]Glen D. Cole, *The Truth About Divorce and Remarriage* (Sacramento: Capital Christian Center, 1982), 9. This booklet was originally a sermon delivered by Cole. Subsequent references to Glen D. Cole are also from this source.

[3]Calvin, as quoted by Barrett, *Corinthians,* 185.

Chapter 4. Jesus on Divorce

[1]John MacArthur, *John MacArthur's Bible Studies on Divorce* (Chicago: Moody Press, 1985), 48. Subsequent references to John MacArthur are also from this source.

Chapter 5. Remarriage: Restrictions

[1]John Dillenberger, ed., *Martin Luther—Selections from His Writings* (Garden City, N.Y.: Doubleday & Company, Inc., 1961), 159.

Chapter 6. Remarriage: Exceptions

[1]James Strong, *Strong's Exhaustive Concordance of the Bible,* "Greek Dictionary" (McLean, Va.: MacDonald Publishing Company, 1890), 24. Subsequent references to James Strong are also from this source.

Chapter 7. Membership

[1]Joseph R. Flower, General Secretary of the Assemblies of God, letter to author.

[2]Cole to author, 18 November 1987.

[3]P. 18. Cole's comment of which ministries are open to the remarried was simply stating what is *commonly* the case among Assemblies of God churches. He, however, goes on to take issue with the narrow limitation of the Assemblies of God position.

Chapter 8. Annulments

[1]"Position on Divorce and Remarriage Upheld by General Council," *Pentecostal Evangel,* 2 October 1983, 12, emphasis added.

Bibliography

Books

Adams, Jay E. *Marriage, Divorce, and Remarriage.* Grand Rapids: Baker Book House, 1980.

Barrett, C. K. *The First Epistle to the Corinthians.* Harper's New Testament Commentaries. New York: Harper & Row, 1968.

Cosby, Michael R. *Sex in the Bible.* Englewood Cliffs, N.J.: Prentice Hall, Inc., 1984.

Dillenberger, John, ed. *Martin Luther—Selections from His Writings.* Garden City, N.Y.: Doubleday & Company, Inc., 1961.

Dobson, Edward G. *What the Bible Really Says About Marriage, Divorce and Remarriage.* Old Tappan, N.J.: Fleming H. Revell Company, 1986.

Elwell, Walter A., ed., *Evangelical Dictionary of Theology.* Grand Rapids: Baker Book House, 1984.

MacArthur, John. *John MacArthur's Bible Studies on Divorce.* Chicago: Moody Press, 1985.

Morris, Leon. *The First Epistle of Paul to the Corinthians,* Vol. 7. Tyndale New Testament Commentaries. Grand Rapids: Wm. B. Eerdmans, 1981.

Pickthorn, William E., ed. *Minister's Manual.* Vol. 2, "Services for Weddings and Funerals." Springfield, Mo.: Gospel Publishing House, 1965.

Richards, Larry. *Remarriage: A Healing Gift From God.* Waco, Tex.: Word Books, 1981.

Small, Dwight Hervey. *The Right to Remarry.* Old Tappan, N.J.: Fleming H. Revell Company, 1977.

Strong, James. *Strong's Exhaustive Concordance of the Bible.* McLean, Va.: MacDonald Publishing Company, 1890.

Vine, W. E., Unger, Merrill F., and White, William Jr. *An Expos-*

itory Dictionary of Biblical Words. Nashville: Thomas Nelson Publishers, 1984.

Wight, Fred H. *Manners and Customs of Bible Lands.* Chicago: Moody Press, 1953.

Periodicals

Dobbins, Richard. "Divorce: Permitted But Not Prescribed," *Charisma,* March 1978, 12–15.

"More Divorces, Deaths, and Births, Fewer Marriages in U.S. in 1985, Preliminary Figures Show," *Pentecostal Evangel,* 25 May 1986, 24.

"Number of Divorces Declines Nationwide for First Time in 2 Decades," *Pentecostal Evangel* 5 May 1985, 14.

"Position on Divorce and Remarriage Upheld by General Council," *Pentecostal Evangel,* 2 October 1983, 12.

"Scars of Divorce," *Pentecostal Evangel,* 2 December 1962, 16–17, 21–22.

Miscellaneous

Cole, Frank, Northwest District Superintendent of the Assemblies of God. Letter to author, 18 November 1987.

Cole, Glen. *The Truth About Divorce and Remarriage.* Sacramento: Captial Christian Center, 1982.

"Divorce and Remarriage." Position Paper of the Assemblies of God. Approved August 1973. Springfield, Mo.: Gospel Publishing House, 1987 (order number: 34–4189).

Flower, Joseph R., General Secretary of the Assemblies of God. Letter to author.

Hodges, Jim. "Twelve Pictures of the New Testament Church," Christ for the Nations Institute, Dallas, Texas.

Scripture Index

Subject Index